FIRST 50 CLASSICAL PIECES
YOU SHOULD PLAY ON THE PIANO

ISBN 978-1-4803-9841-2

HAL•LEONARD®
CORPORATION
7777 W. BLUEMOUND RD. P.O. BOX 13819 MILWAUKEE, WI 53213

In Australia Contact:
Hal Leonard Australia Pty. Ltd.
4 Lentara Court
Cheltenham, Victoria, 3192 Australia
Email: ausadmin@halleonard.com.au

Visit Hal Leonard Online at
www.halleonard.com

ARABESQUE
Op. 100, No. 2

By JOHANN FRIEDRICH BURGMÜLLER
(1806–1874)

Allegro scherzando

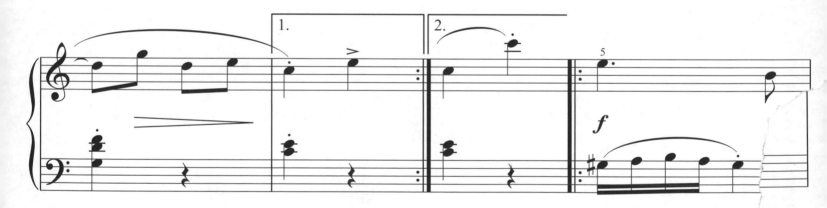

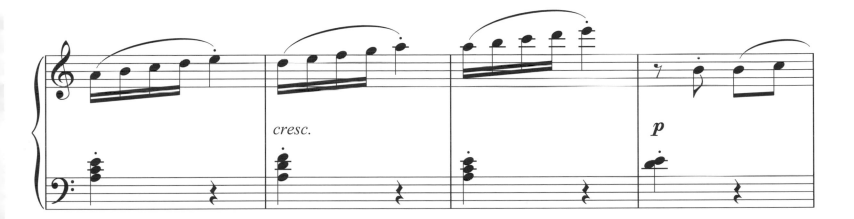

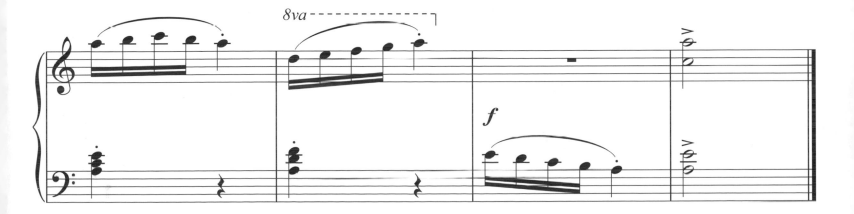

ARIOSO
from CANTATA NO. 156

By JOHANN SEBASTIAN BACH
(1685–1750)

5

6

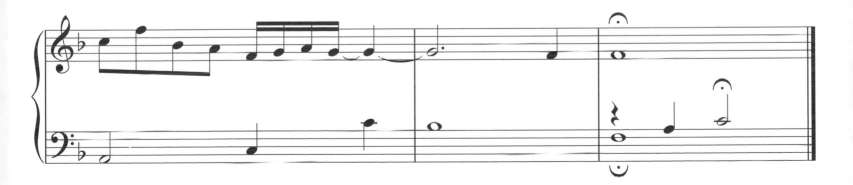

AVE MARIA

By FRANZ SCHUBERT
(1797–1828)

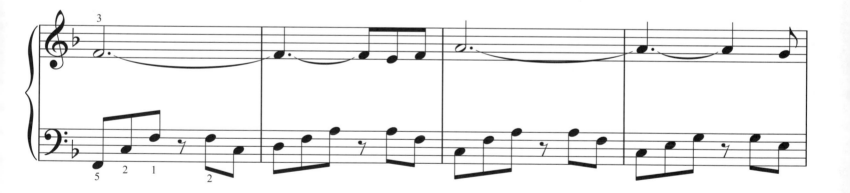

- page 9

CAN CAN
from ORPHEUS IN THE UNDERWORLD

By JACQUES OFFENBACH
(1819–1880)

Allegro

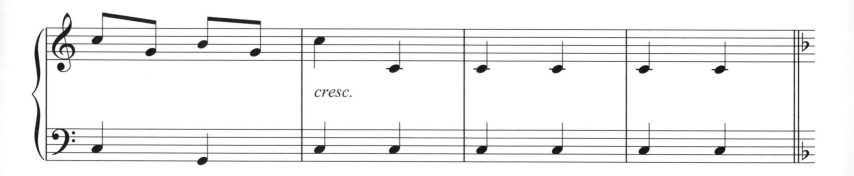

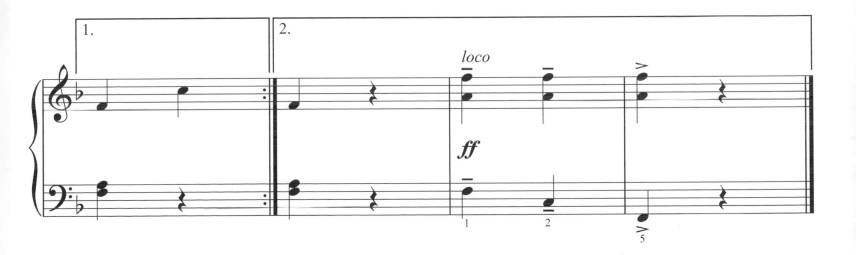

CANON IN D

By JOHANN PACHELBEL
(1653–1706)

Slowly

mp

With pedal

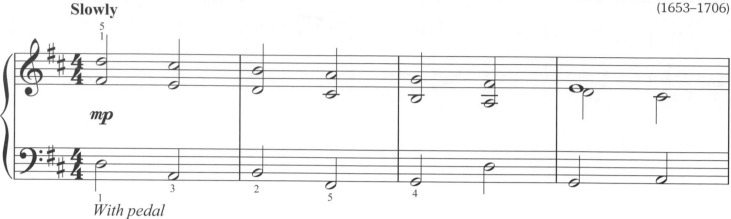

CLAIR DE LUNE

By CLAUDE DEBUSSY
(1862–1918)

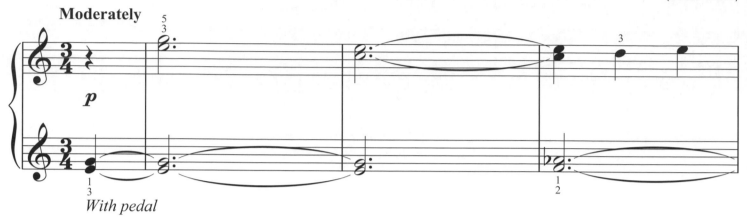

With pedal

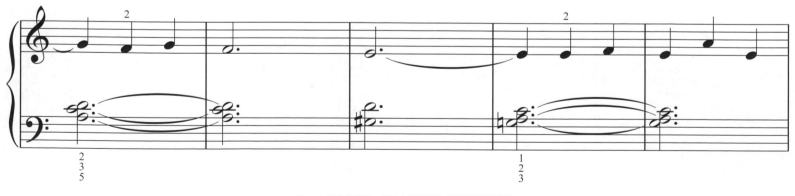

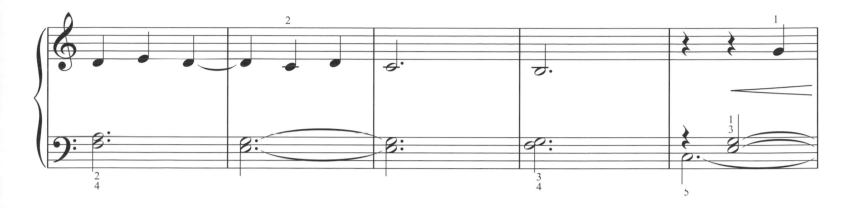

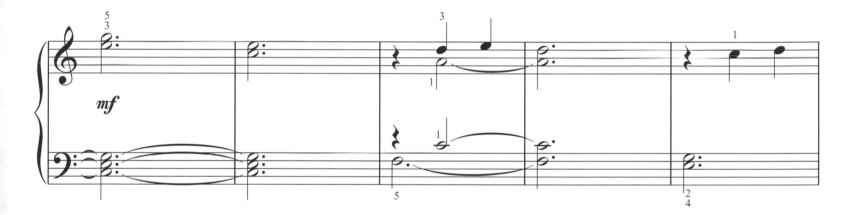

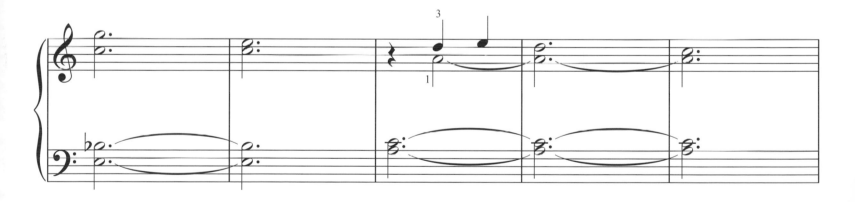

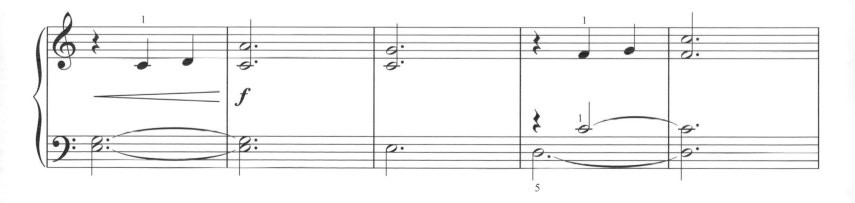

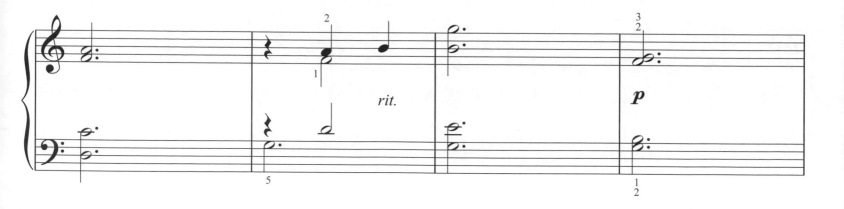

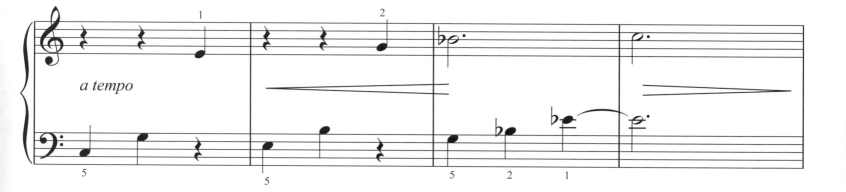

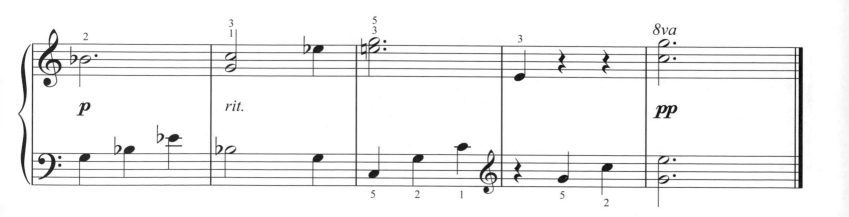

FUNERAL MARCH
from Piano Sonata in B-flat Minor, Op. 35

By FREDERIC CHOPIN
(1810–1849)

EINE KLEINE NACHTMUSIK

By WOLFGANG AMADEUS MOZART
(1756–1791)

Moderately fast

FANTASIE IMPROMPTU
(Theme)

By FREDERIC CHOPIN
(1810–1849)

FÜR ELISE

By LUDWIG VAN BEETHOVEN
(1770–1827)

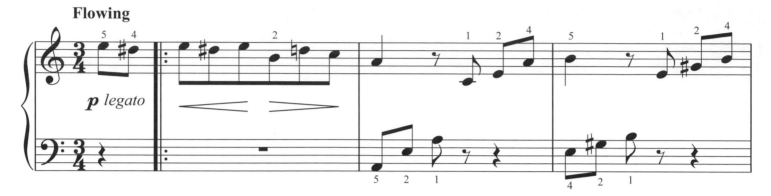

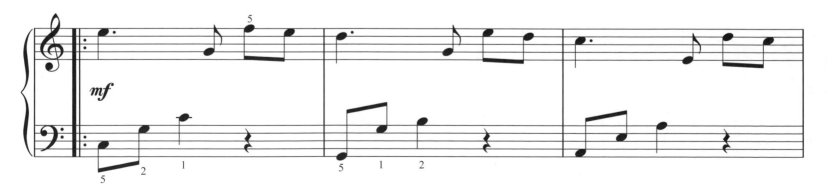

GYMNOPÉDIE NO. 1

By ERIK SATIE
(1866–1925)

Slowly and sadly

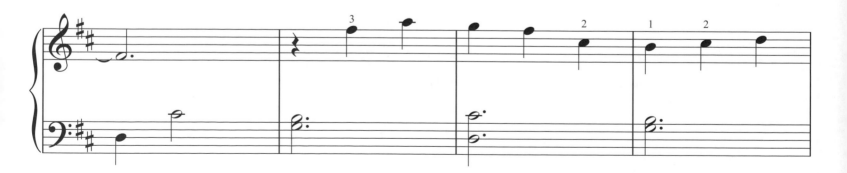

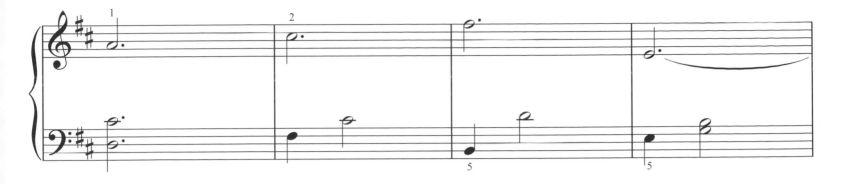

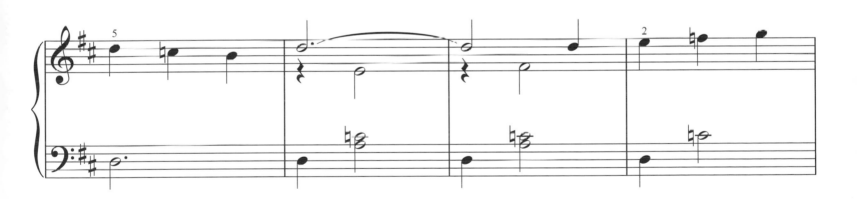

To Coda $\oplus$

D.C. al Coda

CODA

HABANERA
from CARMEN

By GEORGES BIZET
(1838–1875)

Allegretto quasi Andantino, in 2

With pedal

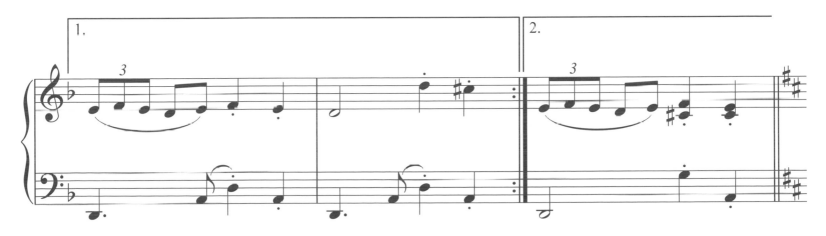

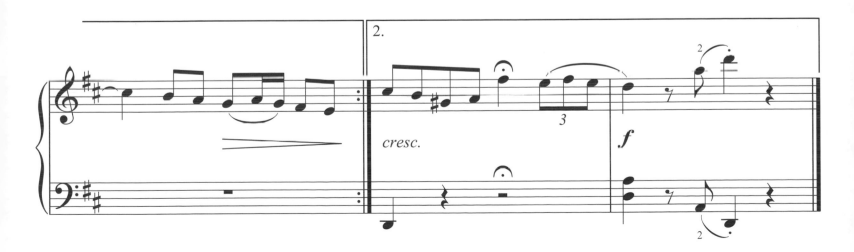

HALLELUJAH CHORUS
from MESSIAH

By GEORGE FRIDERIC HANDEL
(1685–1759)

Majestically

THE HAPPY FARMER

By ROBERT SCHUMANN
(1810–1856)

Moderately fast

HUMORESQUE

By ANTONÍN DVOŘÁK
(18841–1904)

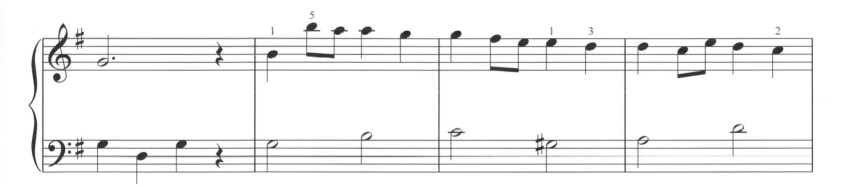

D.C. al Coda

CODA

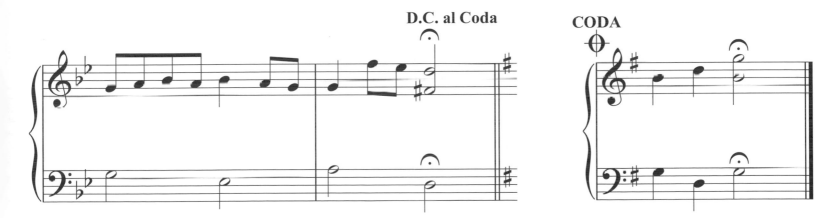

HUNGARIAN DANCE NO. 5

By JOHANNES BRAHMS
(1833–1897)

Fast, with passion

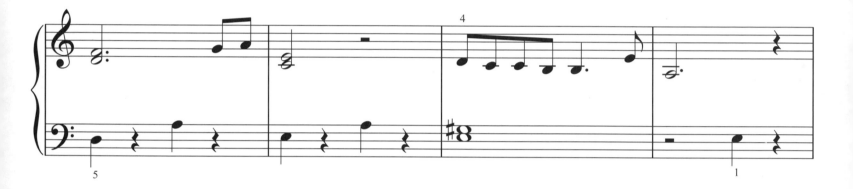

Fine

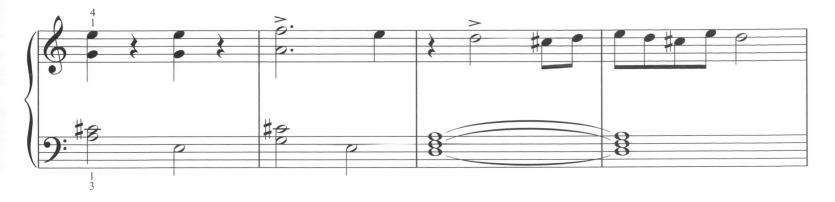

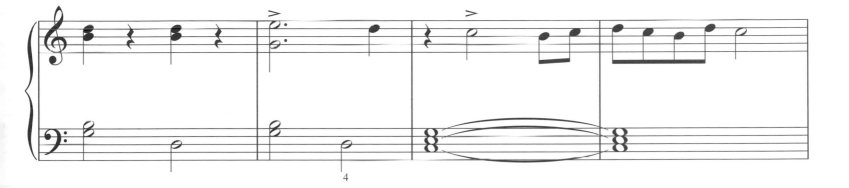

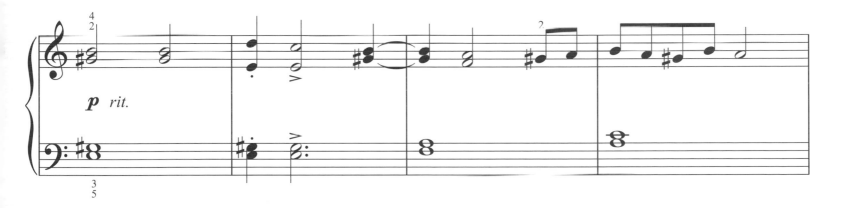

D.C. al Fine
(no repeat)

IN THE HALL OF THE MOUNTAIN KING

from PEER GYNT

By EDVARD GRIEG
(1843–1907)

March

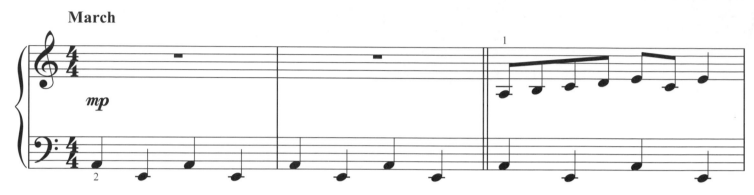

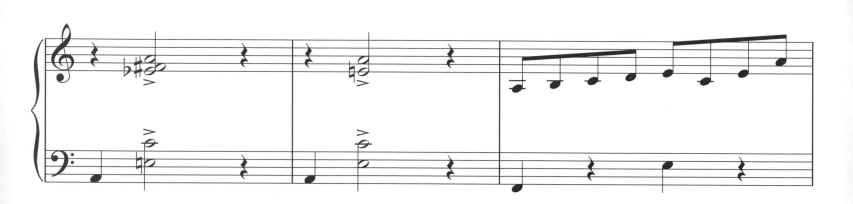

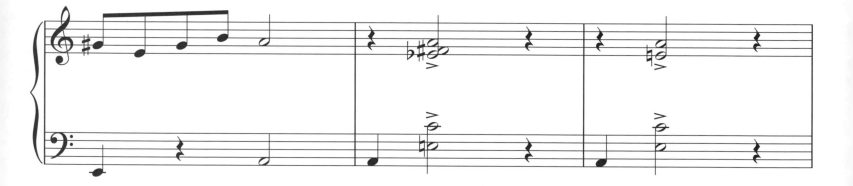

JESU, JOY OF MAN'S DESIRING

By JOHANN SEBASTIAN BACH
(1685–1750)

Andante cantabile

LA DONNA È MOBILE
from RIGOLETTO

By GIUSEPPE VERDI
(1813–1901)

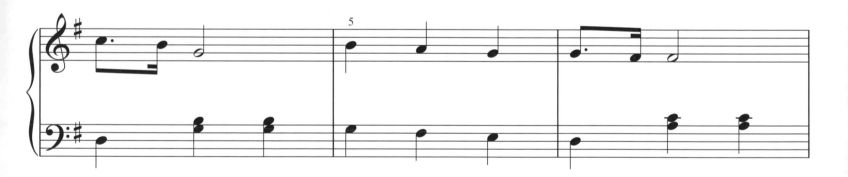

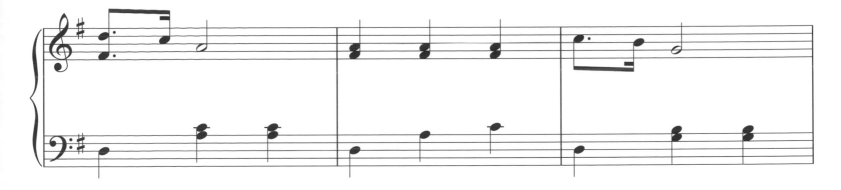

LA FILLE AUX CHEVEUX DE LIN
(The Girl with the Flaxen Hair)

By CLAUDE DEBUSSY
(1862–1918)

Calm, with expression

With pedal

LARGO FROM SYMPHONY NO. 9
("New World")

By ANTONIN DVOŘÁK
(1841–1904)

Largo

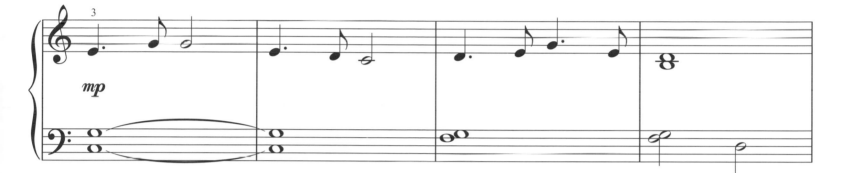

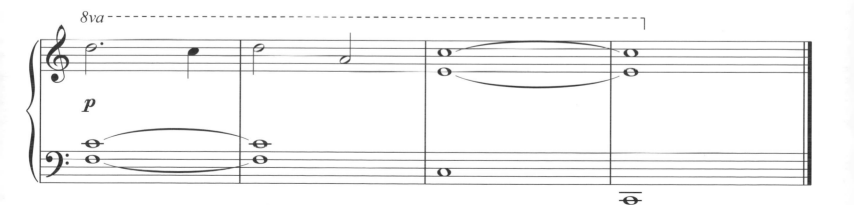

LIEBESTRAUM
(Dream of Love)

By FRANZ LISZT
(1811–1886)

Poco allegro

With pedal

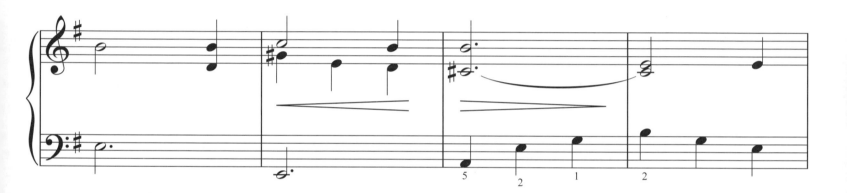

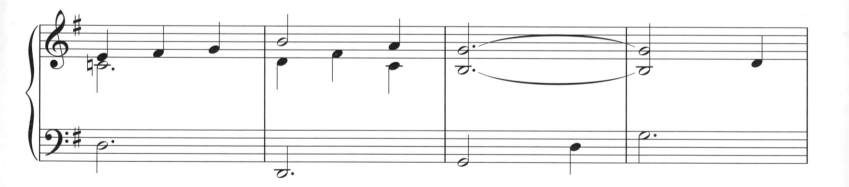

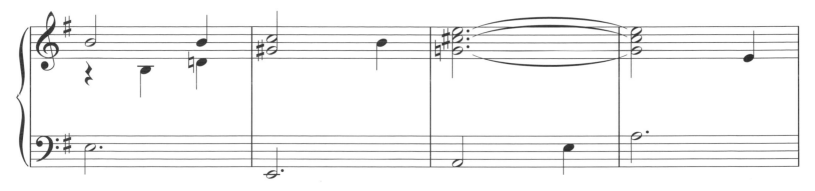

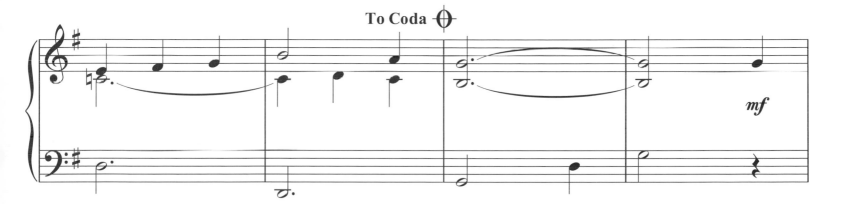

To Coda ⊕

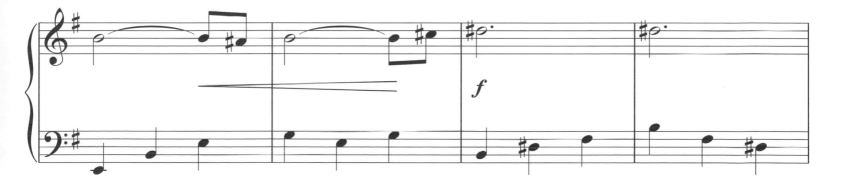

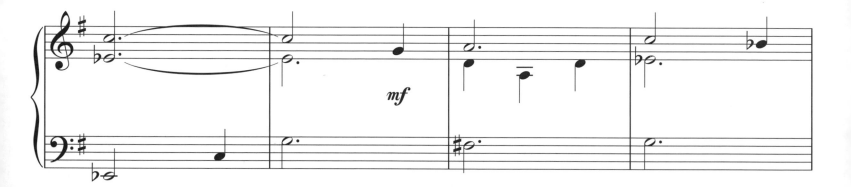

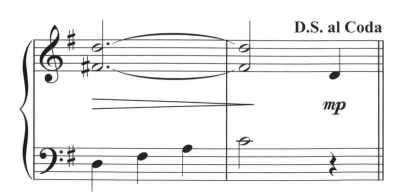

CODA

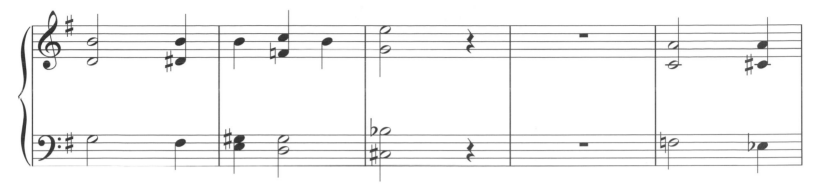

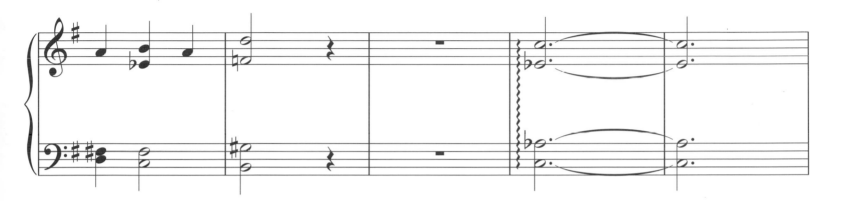

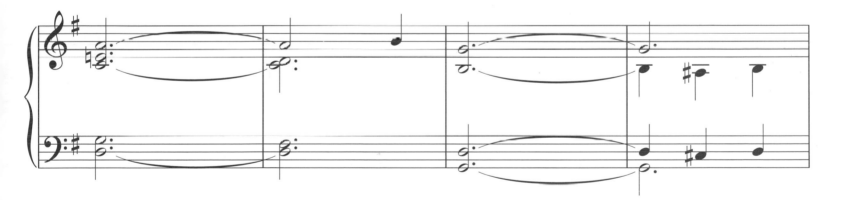

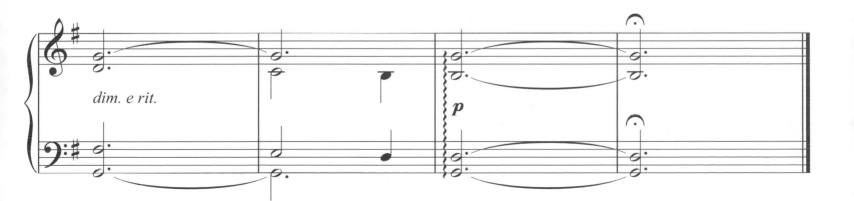

LULLABY
(Cradle Song)

By JOHANNES BRAHMS
(1833–1897)

Tenderly

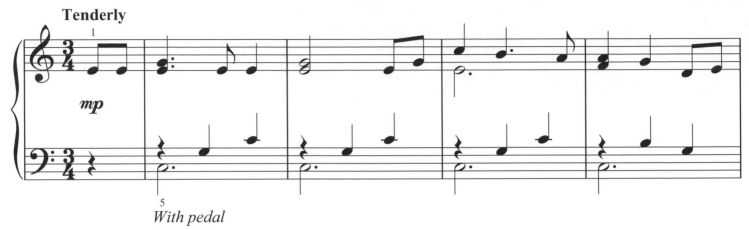

mp

With pedal

MINUET IN G MAJOR

By LUDWIG VAN BEETHOVEN
(1770–1827)

Allegretto

MARCH
from THE NUTCRACKER

By PYOTR IL'YICH TCHAIKOVSKY
(1840–1893)

Moderately, in 2

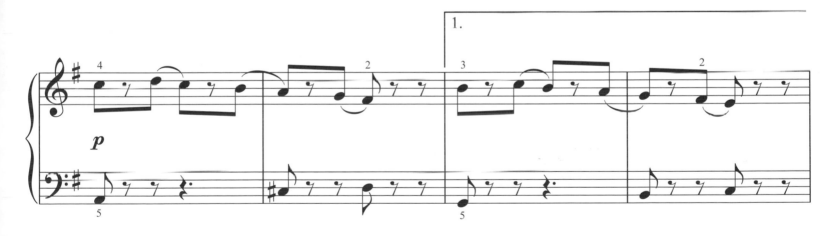

64

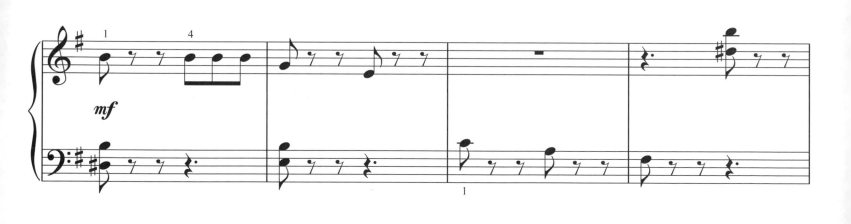

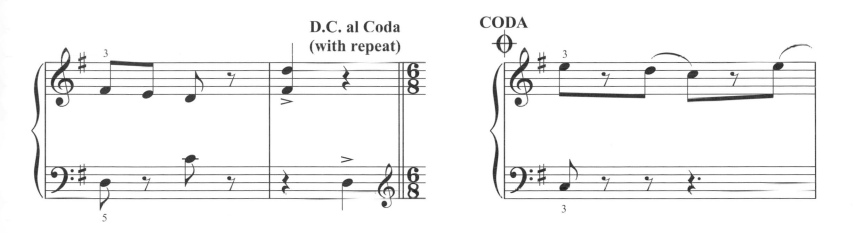

MEDITATION
from THAÏS

By JULES MASSENET
(1842–1912)

Moderately slow

67

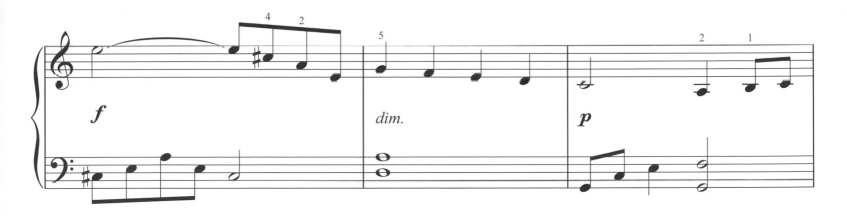

To Coda ⊕

A little faster

Calmly

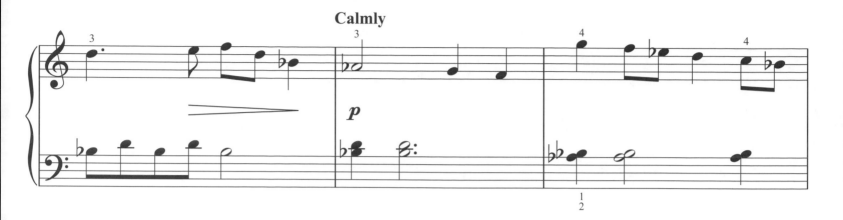

dim. e rit.

D.C. al Coda

CODA

MINUET IN G
from THE ANNA MAGDALENA NOTEBOOK

By JOHANN SEBASTIAN BACH
(1685–1750)

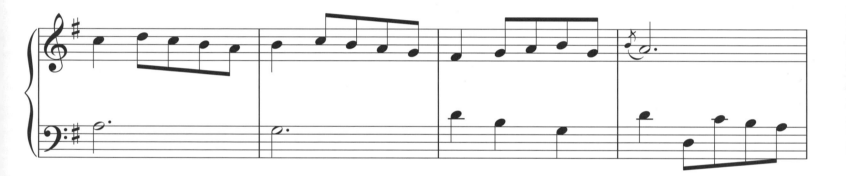

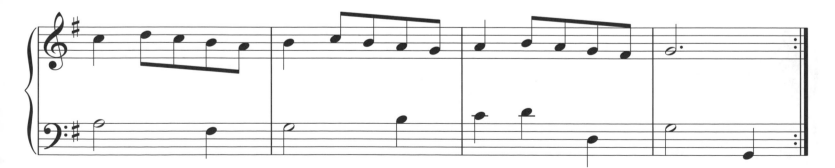

"MOONLIGHT" SONATA IN C# MINOR
Op. 27 No. 2 First Movement Theme

By LUDWIG VAN BEETHOVEN
(1770–1827)

Adagio

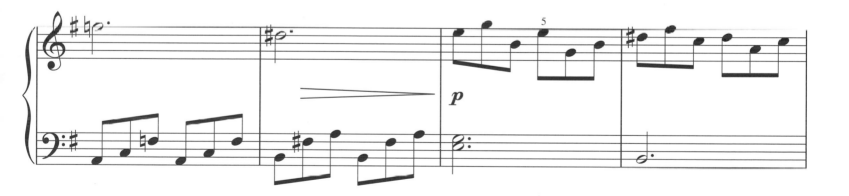

MORNING
from PEER GYNT

By EDVARD GRIEG
(1843–1907)

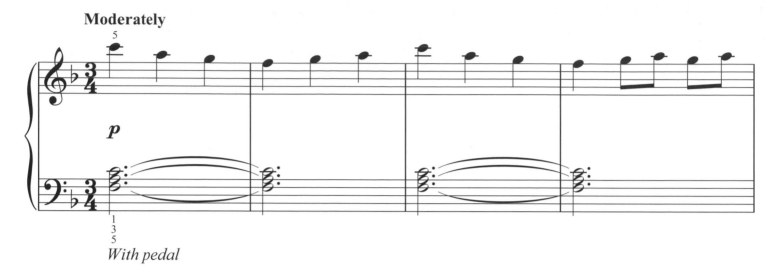

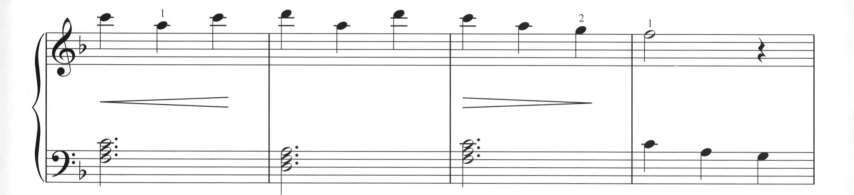

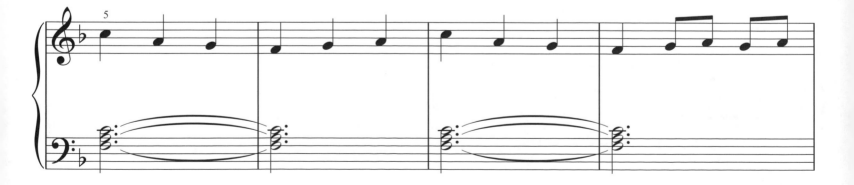

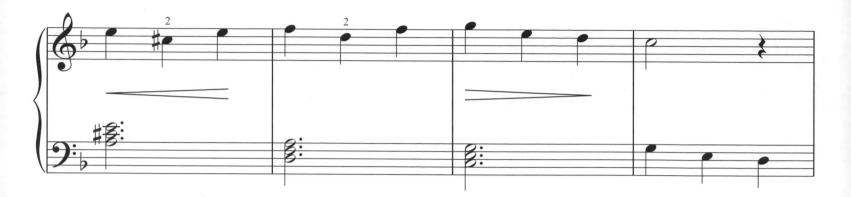

NIGHT ON BALD MOUNTAIN

By MODEST MUSSORGSKY
(1839–1881)

POLOVTSIAN DANCE THEME

By ALEXANDER BORODIN
(1833–1887)

Moderately

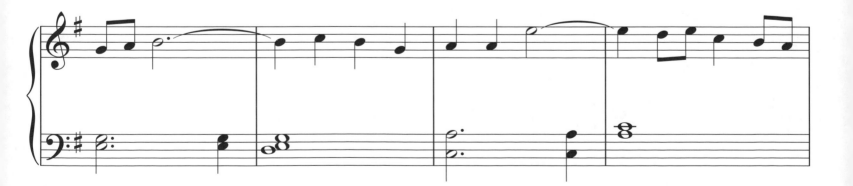

D.C. al Coda

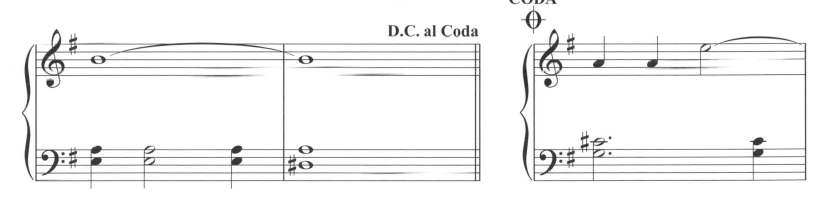

NOCTURNE IN E FLAT MAJOR
Op. 9, No. 2

By FREDERIC CHOPIN
(1810–1849)

Slowly, in 1

ODE TO JOY
from SYMPHONY NO. 9 in D Minor, Fourth Movement Choral Theme

By LUDWIG VAN BEETHOVEN
(1770–1827)

Majestically

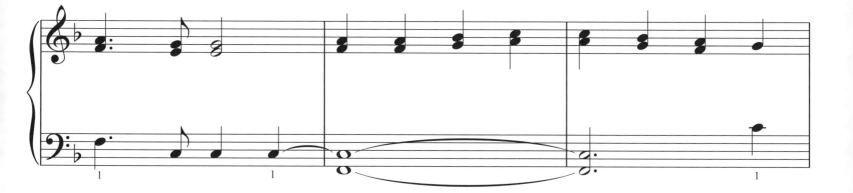

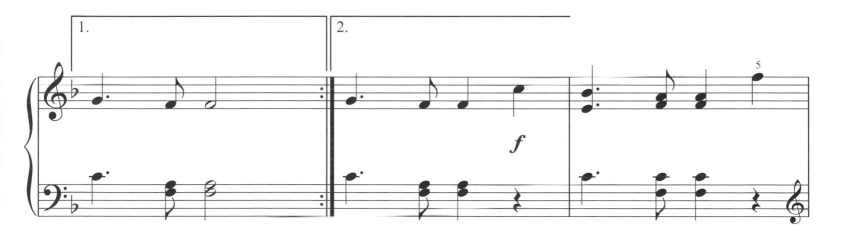

PAVANE POUR UNE INFANTE DEFUNTE

By MAURICE RAVEL
(1875–1937)

Slowly

mp

With pedal

rit.

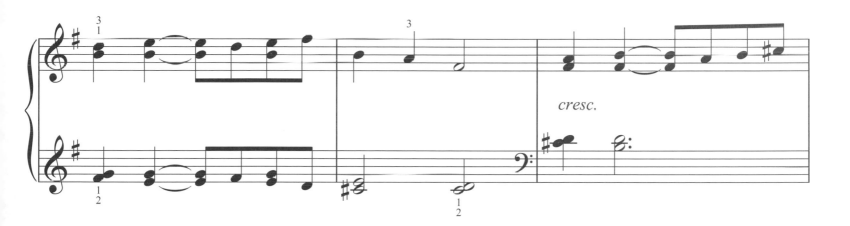

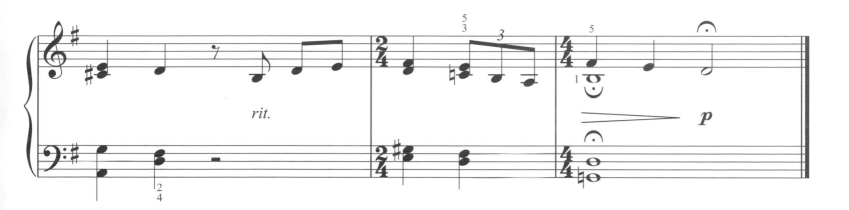

PIANO CONCERTO NO. 2
Third Movement Excerpt

By SERGEI RACHMANINOFF
(1873–1943)

Moderately, with expression

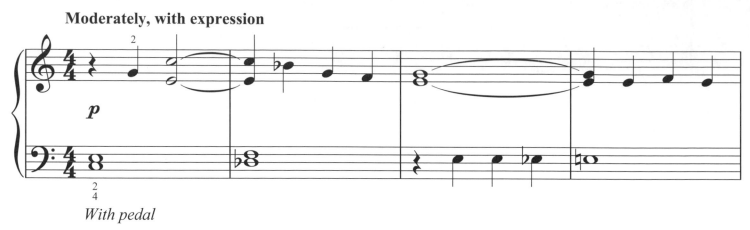

With pedal

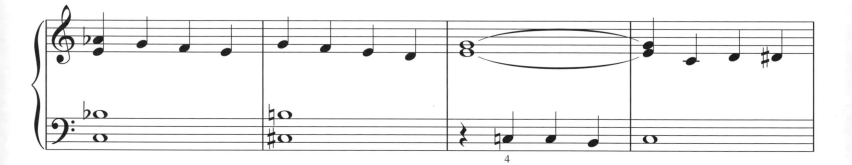

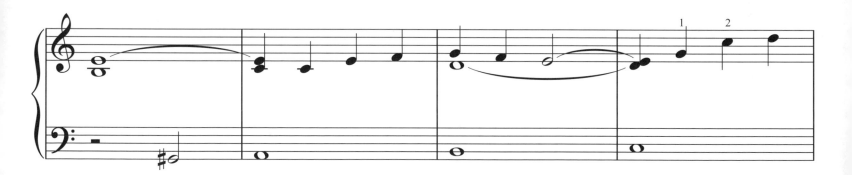

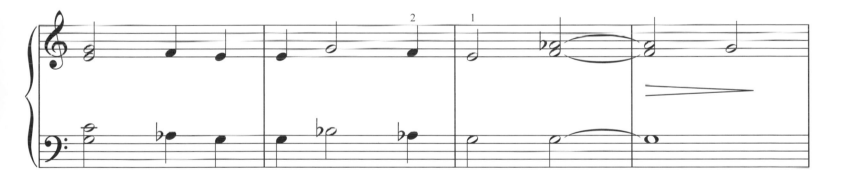

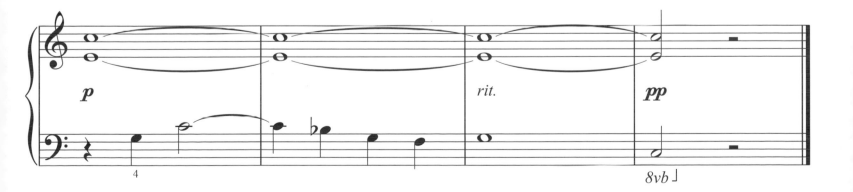

PICTURES AT AN EXHIBITION
(Theme)

By MODEST MUSSORGSKY
(1839–1881)

RÊVERIE

By CLAUDE DEBUSSY
(1862–1918)

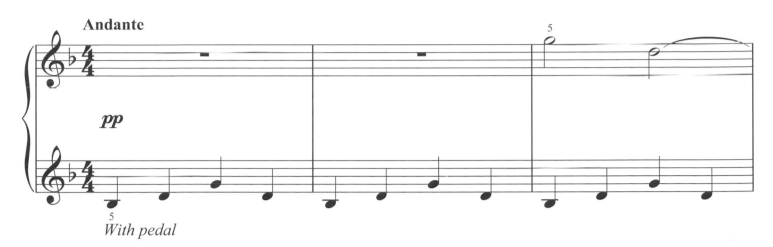

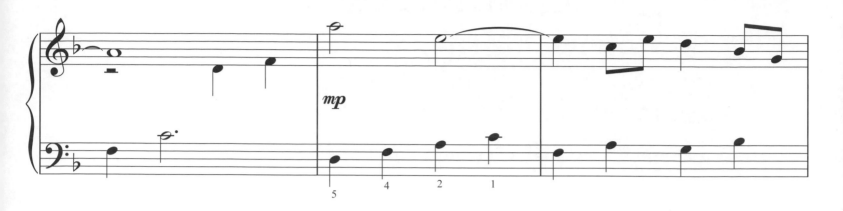

POMP AND CIRCUMSTANCE

By EDWARD ELGAR
(1857–1934)

With dignity

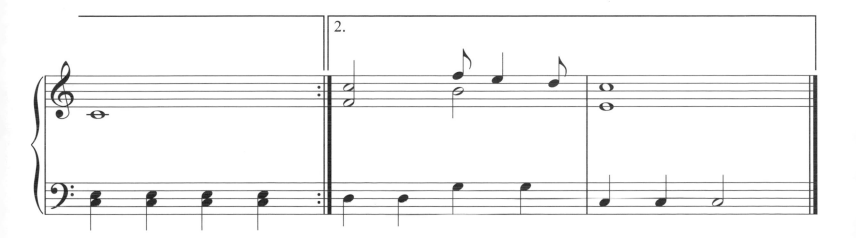

RHAPSODY ON A THEME OF PAGANINI
Variation XVIII

By SERGEI RACHMANINOFF
(1873–1943)

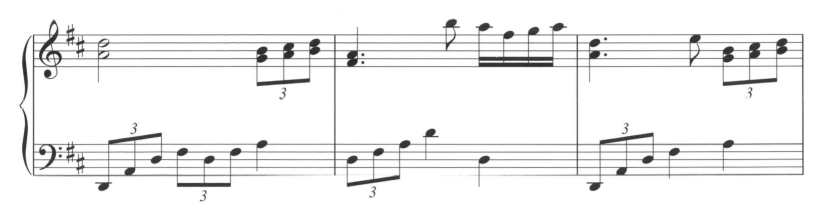

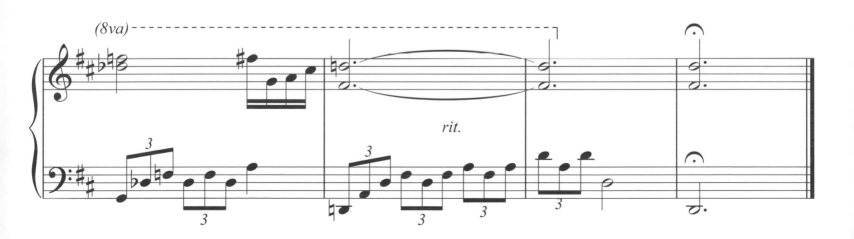

ROMEO AND JULIET
(Love Theme)

By PYOTR IL'YICH TCHAIKOVSKY
(1840–1893)

Andante, con espressione

With pedal

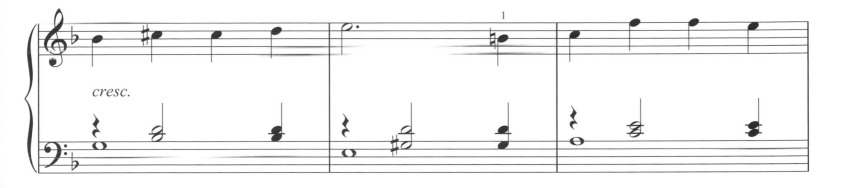

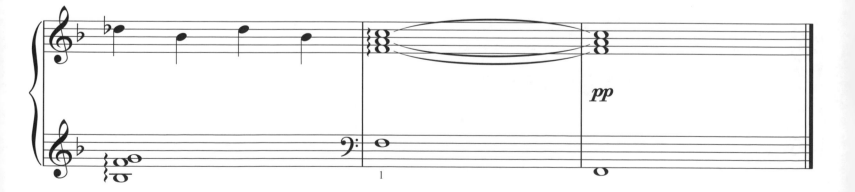

SICILIENNE

By GABRIEL FAURÉ
(1845–1924)

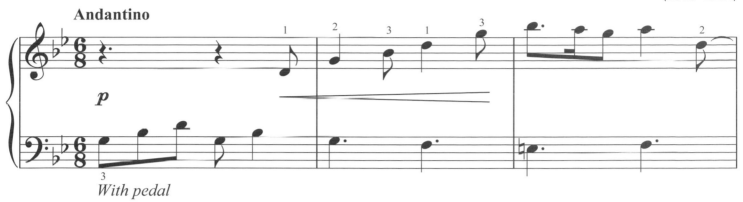

108

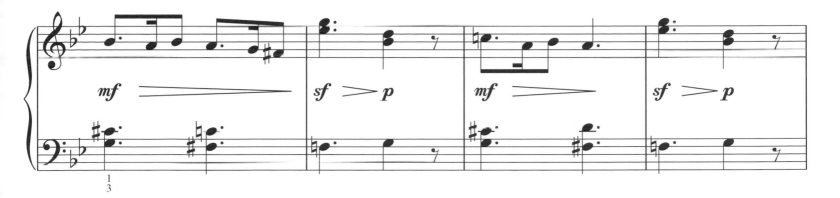

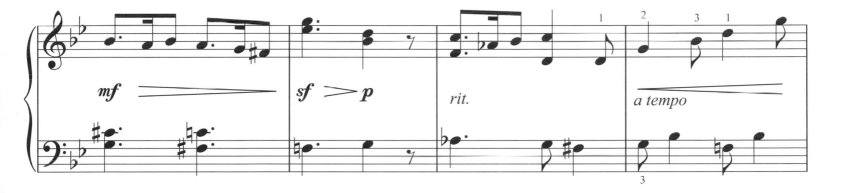

SONATINA IN C MAJOR
Op. 36, No. 1 (First Movement)

By MUZIO CLEMENTI
(1752–1832)

Allegro

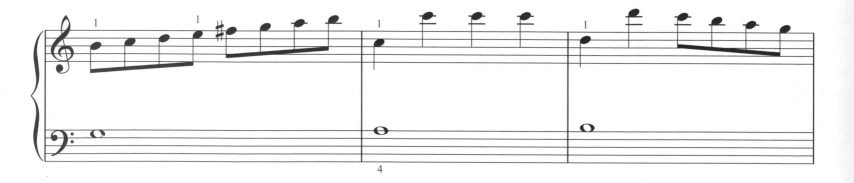

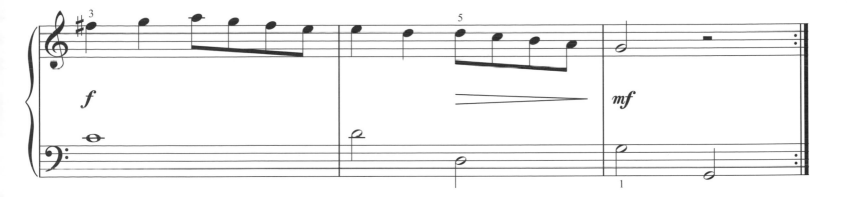

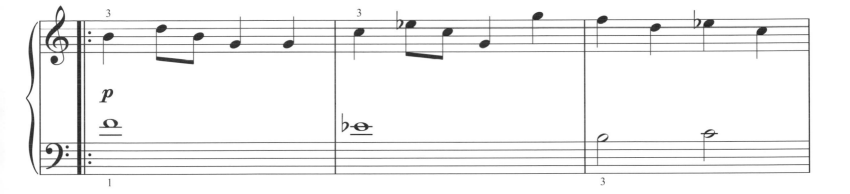

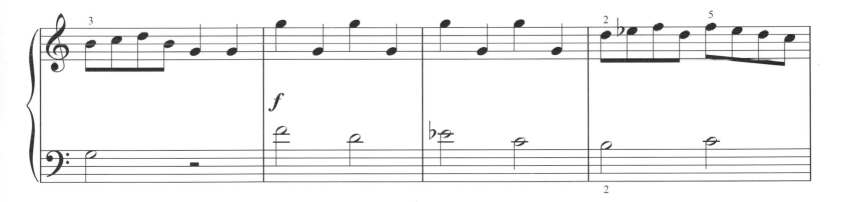

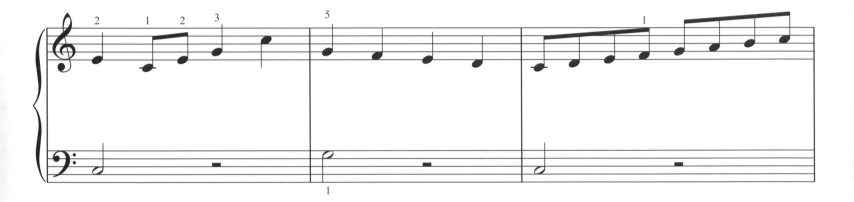

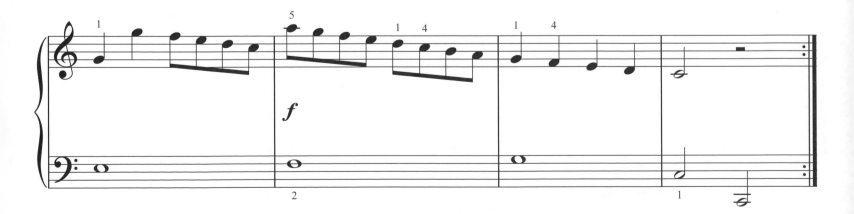

SONATA IN C MAJOR

K. 545, First Movement

By WOLFGANG AMADEUS MOZART
(1756–1791)

Allegro

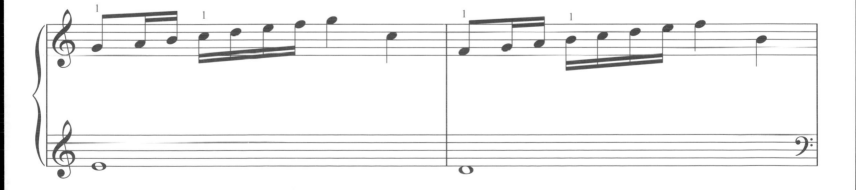

SONATA NO. 11 IN A MAJOR
K 331, Third Movement ("Rondo alla Turca")

By WOLFGANG AMADEUS MOZART
(1756–1791)

Allegretto

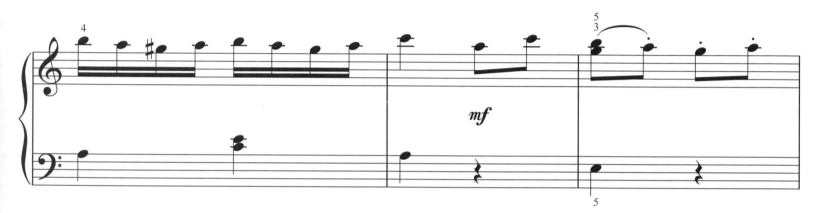

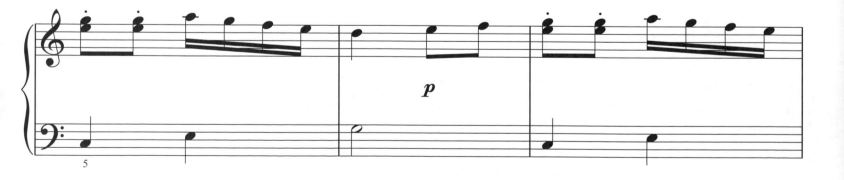

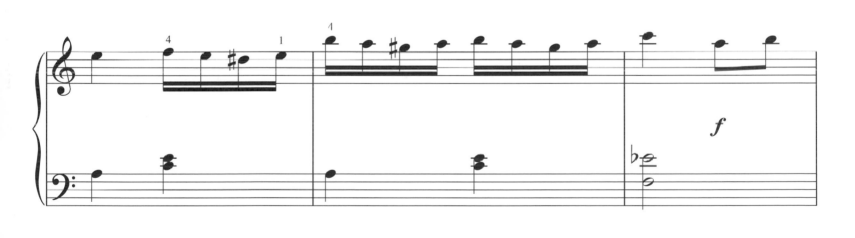

SPINNING SONG

By ALBERT ELLMENREICH
(1816–1905)

Allegretto

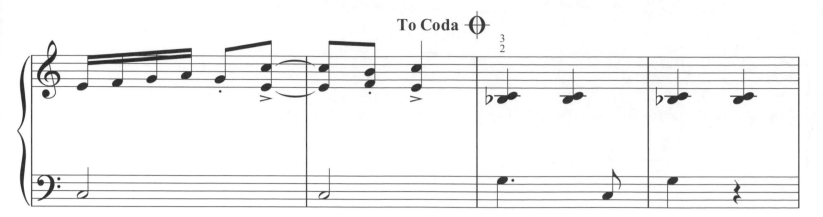

To Coda ⊕

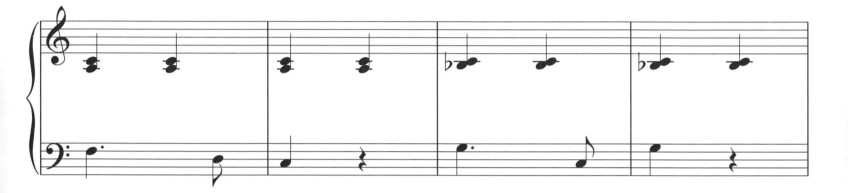

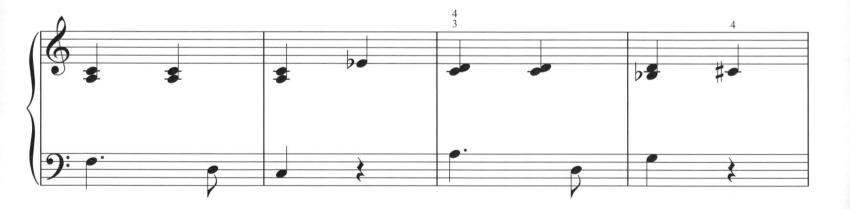

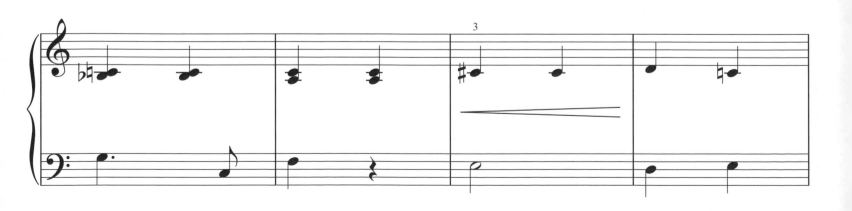

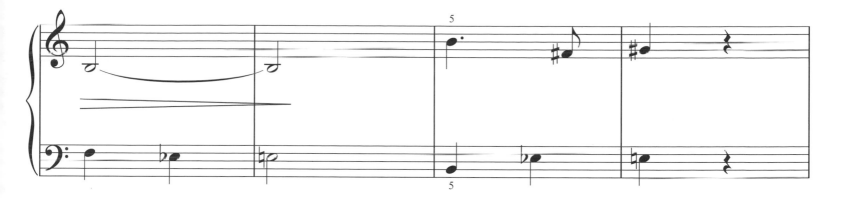

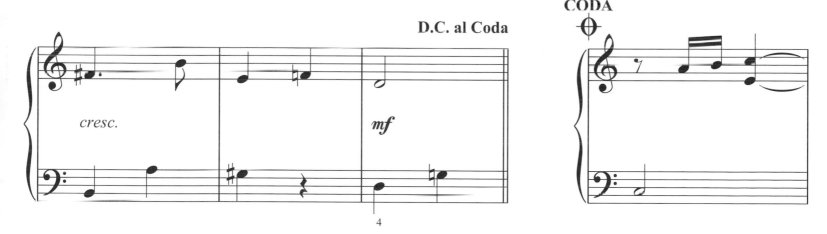

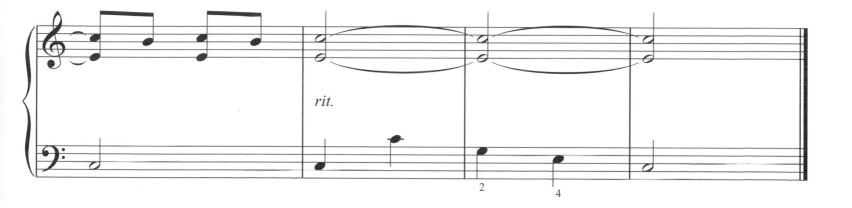

THE SURPRISE SYMPHONY

By FRANZ JOSEPH HAYDN
(1732–1809)

Moderately slow

THE SWAN
(Le Cygne)
from CARNIVAL OF THE ANIMALS

By CAMILLE SAINT-SAËNS
(1835–1921)

Slowly

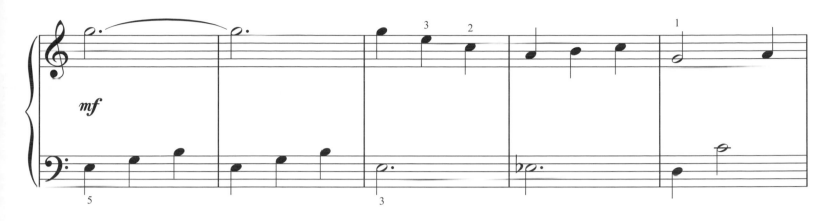

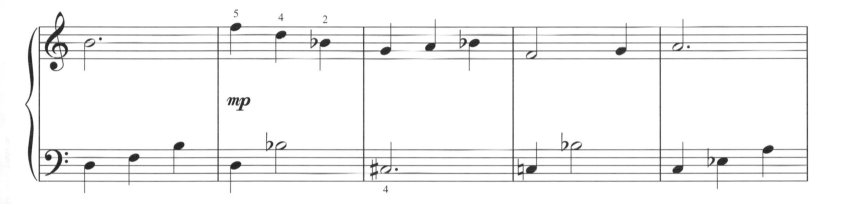

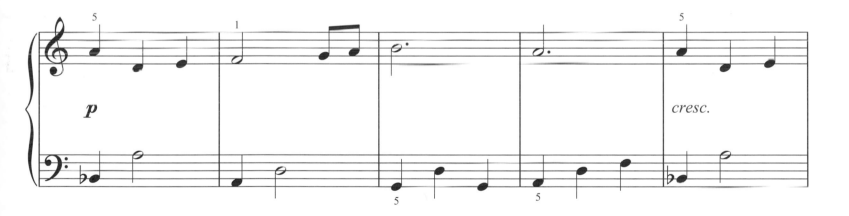

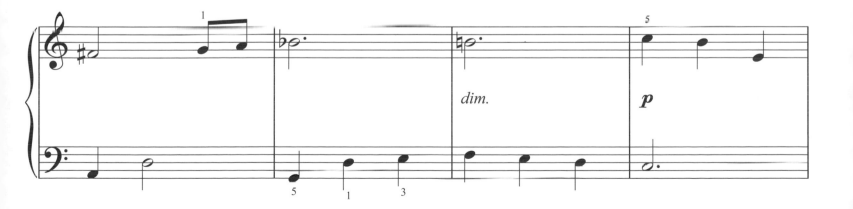

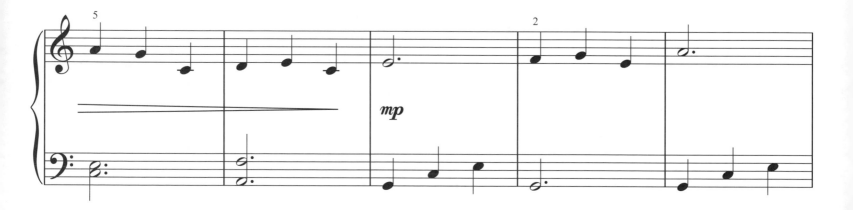

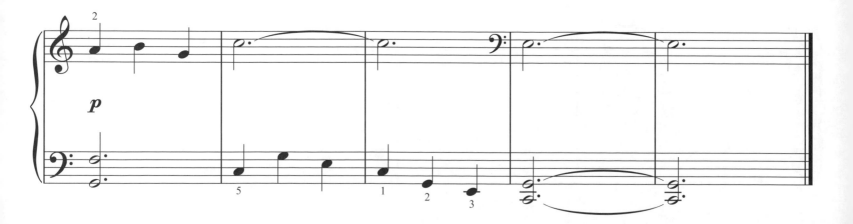

TO A WILD ROSE
from WOODLAND SKETCHES

By EDWARD MacDOWELL
(1860–1908)

With simple tenderness

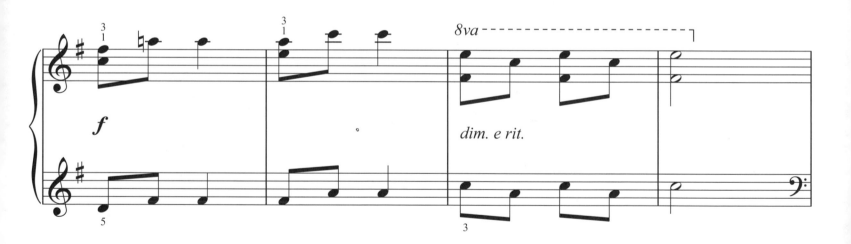

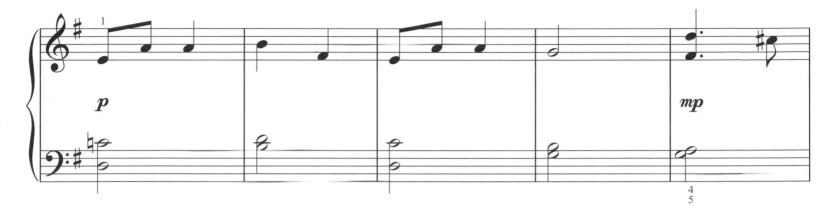

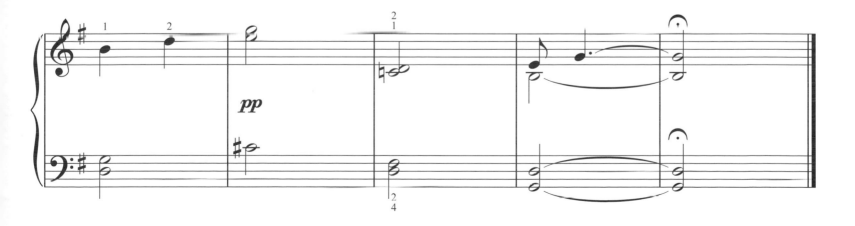

WALTZ IN A MINOR

By FREDERIC CHOPIN
(1810–1849)

Allegretto

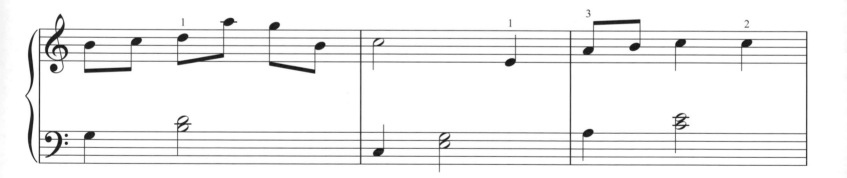

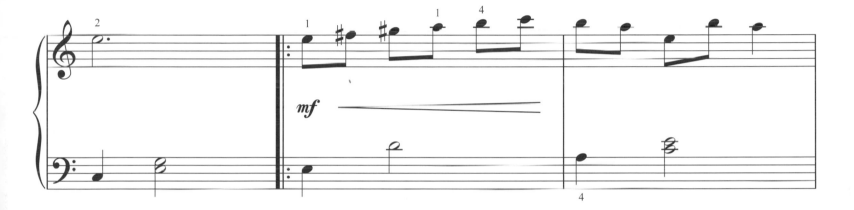

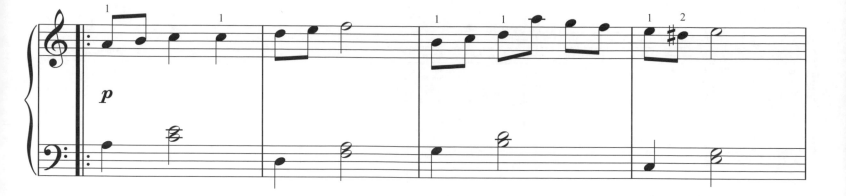

WILLIAM TELL OVERTURE

featured in the TV Series THE LONE RANGER

By GIOVANNI ROSSINI
(1792–1868)

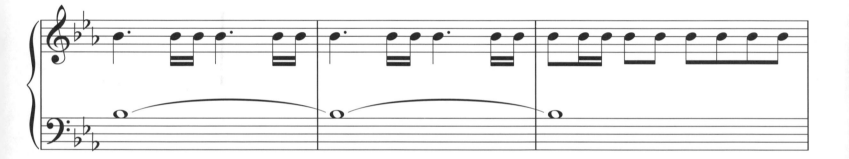

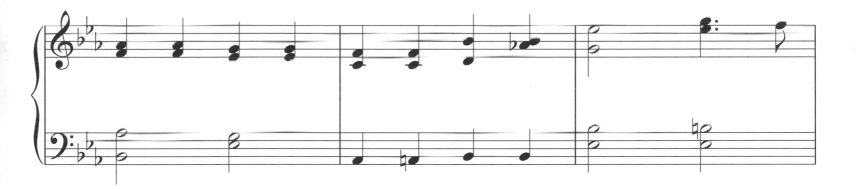

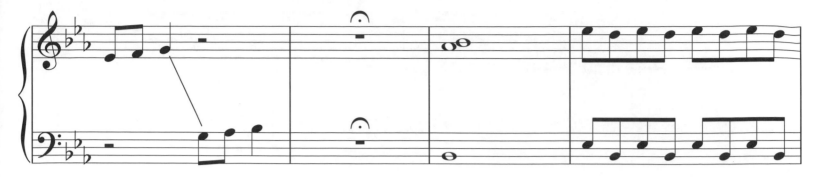